Original title:
The Carnation Chronicle

Copyright © 2025 Creative Arts Management OÜ
All rights reserved.

Author: Seraphina Caldwell
ISBN HARDBACK: 978-1-80566-742-1
ISBN PAPERBACK: 978-1-80566-871-8

Echoes of a Floral Journey

Once a flower danced in shoes,
It twirled and swayed, singing the blues.
But every jig led to a sprout,
And petals laughed, 'Oh, look who's out!'

A bee passed by, with a buzzing cheer,
Said, "Buddy, stick to drinks, not beer!"
But the flower sipped on sweet nectar,
"I'm just chilling, no need for a lecture!"

Chronicles of the Crimson Bloom

A bold red bloom, so ostentatious,
Pulled pranks on buds, oh how fantastious!
"I'm the beauty, crown me, please!"
While daffodils giggled behind the trees.

With each sunset, it donned a hat,
Wore a sunflower as a simple sprat.
"Look at me!" it shouted with glee,
While roses just rolled, 'Oh, let it be!'

Reveries of the Floral Muse

In a garden where daisies play chess,
A sunflower sat, saying, "I'm the best!"
But petals flicked and chlorophyll sighed,
"No one's winning, just growing outside!"

Lily twirled with a fragrant grace,
While thorns came in with a prickly face.
"Play nice, dear friends," the tulips sang,
As rocks chimed in with a chuckle, "Clang!"

A Symphony of Color and Scent

A bouquet formed a quirky band,
With violets strumming, isn't it grand?
While marigolds clapped, petals in tune,
Singing 'Under the Blossoms, we light up the moon!'

Daisies shouted, "That's offbeat!"
But roses twirled on their glorious feet.
"Let's keep it wild, no rules tonight!
We're flowers at heart; we'll be alright!"

Blooming in Silence

In a garden full of chatter,
A flower tried to speak,
But all it could do was stutter,
It bloomed from week to week.

The daisies giggled loud,
The roses rolled their eyes,
The tulips formed a crowd,
While violets just sighed.

With every toss of breeze,
It danced quite out of tune,
Yet laughter came with ease,
Underneath the silvery moon.

So here's a little wink,
To blooms that can't express,
They nod and laugh, I think,
In their own floral mess.

Stories that Blossom

Once a bud with dreams so grand,
Told tales of bees and fun,
But tangled roots did strand,
It couldn't even run.

A sunflower caught its tale,
And rolled it with delight,
But winds began to flail,
And scattered words in flight.

Petals perked, they leaned in close,
For every story spun,
But giggles soon arose,
As blooms would dodge the sun.

So next time you catch a glance,
At colors soft and bright,
Remember blooms just want a chance,
To share their joyful plight!

Colors that Speak

In hues of pink and yellow,
They whisper on the breeze,
Each petal is a fellow,
With secrets to appease.

The orange ones boast bold,
While blues are coolly shy,
A purple fights the mold,
As brown just wants to fly.

Together they collide,
In a riot of delight,
Their painted smiles can't hide,
Each giggle taking flight.

So take a stroll, and see,
Colors having fun,
You might just hear their glee,
As they dance beneath the sun.

The Memory of Petals

Once there bloomed a dandy,
Whose charm was quite a hoot,
It sported petals handy,
As wild as day-old fruit.

The petals dropped like notes,
Each memory a song,
They flapped like little boats,
As laughter came along.

A daffodil took flight,
Slightly swayed with glee,
A whirly twirl of light,
Became a memory.

So if you're feeling low,
Just glance at blooms near you,
Their giggles gently flow,
Creating joy anew.

Echoes of Floral Memories

In the garden, blooms did chatter,
Petals pranced, oh, what a clatter!
Butterflies wore silly hats,
Dancing with giggling chitchats.

Bees buzzed songs of old romance,
While daisies joined this wacky dance.
Tulips told their knock-knock jokes,
As purple pansies played like folks.

The Unfolding Story

A rose declared, "I'm quite the star!"
"I bloom at parties, yes, by far!"
But daisies rolled their eyes and sighed,
"Aw, come on, don't let it go to your pride!"

Chrysanths chimed in, dancing around,
"Look at me! I'm the sassy crown!"
But laughter erupted from all around,
In this floral tale where jokes abound.

In the Garden of Dreams

In dreams, the flowers softly glow,
With whispers that only petals know.
They tell of secrets, silly and sweet,
Of spilled lemonade and dancing feet.

Lilies giggle as they sway,
"What's a flower's favorite play?"
"Why, it's 'Petal Pals,' don't you see?
The funniest show, just wait for me!"

Fragrance of Forgotten Days

Once in a pot, a cactus sighed,
"I wish I had the flowers' ride!"
But violets chuckled, "Don't you fret,
Cacti parties? The best you'll get!"

Laughter echoed through sunlit rays,
As daisies shared their fuzziest days.
"Remember last spring? That bee's big buzz?
He stole my hat—oh, what a fuzz!"

Tales of the Garden Path

Amidst the blooms so bright and bold,
A tale of mischief must be told.
The daisies danced, the roses sighed,
Where butterflies and bees collide.

One morning, weeds pulled off a prank,
They swirled the petals, LEFT 'em blank!
A tulip tripped, fell to the ground,
Said, "Watch your step, we're garden bound!"

The sunflowers laughed, their heads held high,
As ladybugs exchanged a sly eye.
The frogs croaked jokes, the snails were slow,
In this patch of joy, hilarity would grow.

Oh, jesters of greens, with roots so deep,
You splash the garden with laughter and peep.
So raise your spade and join the fun,
In this comedy, we are all one!

A History in Buds

Out from the soil, stories rise,
With petals wide and no disguise.
A daffodil claimed, "I sprouted first!"
While violets giggled, "Oh, we're the worst!"

The old oak tree recalled with glee,
"Once a sunflower challenged me!"
But that swift bloom fell to the ground,
It swayed too much, could not be found.

Ah, stories spun with laughter clear,
As bees buzz by, they stop to cheer.
A daisies' tale of a bee with flair,
He wore such style, with flowers in hair!

And thus the buds continue to bloom,
Sharing their past in the garden room.
With humor stitched among each leaf,
These histories thrive beyond belief!

Petal Poetry

Under the sun, the petals sway,
They whisper secrets of the day.
A buttercup said, "What a sight!"
"Last night's thunder? Pure delight!"

A poppy laughed, "What a big sound!
I thought I'd sprout right from the ground!"
While all the flowers traded their jokes,
The worms just chuckled, real garden folks.

"Why did the rose refuse to bloom?
Because the garden had no room!"
The daisies hooted, and the lilies swayed,
In this petal poetry parade.

And as the sun began to wane,
They sang of sprouts and gentle rain.
With laughter woven 'twixt each row,
Their tales shall flourish, ebb, and flow.

Ode to the Wildflower

Oh wildflower, you blaze so free,
In every nook, you sway with glee.
You sprout where you please, with style so rare,
Even the daisies stop and stare!

With colors bright and scents that tease,
A bumblebee said, "You're such a breeze!"
You dance on hills, you riot in fields,
Your laughter in bloom, all joy it yields.

In cracks of pavement, you find your place,
With giggles and grins, you flaunt your grace.
The gardeners frown, "You can't be here!"
But wildflower knows, it's all cheer, my dear.

To every shade, your presence calls,
You tackle the tough, you conquer it all.
Oh wildflower, with stories galore,
In your funny ways, we always want more!

Petal-Scented Memories

In the garden, bugs all frolic,
They dance around, a funny colonic.
With petals bright, they scheme and plot,
Who eats who? They know a lot.

Lively flowers laugh at clowns,
Wearing pollen hats and funky gowns.
The bees bring news from far and wide,
In this floral crowd, joy cannot hide.

Each bloom's a tale in playful jest,
Their fragrant whispers are the best.
With every breeze, a giggle blooms,
Nature's chuckles, in colorful rooms.

So let us pause, and soak it in,
These petal-scented moments begin.
To share a laugh with every breath,
Life's humor hides beneath the zest.

The Secret Life of Blooms

At dusk, when lights begin to dim,
The flowers dance on a playful whim.
They gossip low in floral tune,
While snails slide past, in the light of the moon.

A daisy winks at a shy rose,
With whispers wrapped in petals' prose.
"Oh darling bud, did you hear the news?
The violets just wore outrageous shoes!"

Butterflies plot their fashion spree,
In colors that make even bees flee.
While crickets play in the grass nearby,
The blooms all cheer, oh, my, oh my!

With every stem, a story grows,
In secret joys that no one knows.
So stretch your leaves and join the show,
Where laughter blooms, and flowers glow.

Traces of Silent Stories

In the shade, the hydrangeas peek,
They catch the sunlight for a cheeky sneak.
Whispering tales of bees and dew,
While butterflies flutter, painting the view.

A tulip tells of weather woes,
Of frosty nights beneath the snows.
The critters giggle at every flub,
While blooms unite in a cozy club.

With every rustle, secrets rise,
As blossoms wink with soft, sly eyes.
They share old jokes with breezy flair,
In a garden filled with vibrant air.

Every petal holds a sassy quip,
From the morning sun, they take a sip.
Join the laughter, let it unfold,
In traces of stories, forever told.

The Unseen Life Beneath

Underneath where roots entwine,
The hidden life is quite divine.
Worms wear hats, all plump and round,
In the dark, their laughter's found.

With underground parties every night,
The fungi dance, such a silly sight.
"Who needs sunlight? We've got style!"
They groove below, going wild.

The beetles keep a silly score,
In this subterranean floor.
With every wiggle, a giggle flows,
As rhizomes riff on garden prose.

So peek below, and dive right in,
You'd find the fun that starts to spin.
In layers deep, the laughter's loud,
Beneath the blooms, we're all so proud.

The Heartbeat of Flowers

In a garden where laughter grows,
A tulip tickles a blushing rose.
With daisies dancing and sparrows chirp,
The sun drops jokes without a quirk.

A lily laughed at a bumblebee,
"You're so fuzzy, come sip tea with me!"
Petunias giggled, sharing a plot,
While dandelions whispered, "Did you hear what they brought?"

A sunflower winked, all golden and bright,
"I'm taller than you, but you still look right!"
Together they bloomed in a colorful spree,
Creating a ruckus, as happy as can be.

In this garden, full of merry sights,
Each petal shares the joy of heights.
With every tickle and every cheer,
The blossoms spread laughter, year after year.

Murmurs from the Blooms

In the shade where the daisies tell tales,
A peony plots outrageous gales.
Roses conspire with violets blue,
Whispering secrets, just me and you.

"Why did the fern cross the path?"
To show off roots and avoid the wrath!
Lilies chuckle at clumsy bees,
"Watch your buzz, don't trip on these leaves!"

Each sunbeam sparkles with a joke,
The orchids giggle, a playful poke.
Mums can't stop with their garden wit,
As zinnias snicker, not giving a bit.

While petals flutter and colors gleam,
These flowers create the silliest dream.
In the garden of glee, where laughter blooms,
Echoes of joy fill the fragrant rooms.

Legends Scarred in Green

Once a weed dreamed it was a tree,
Flapping its leaves, full of glee.
"Look at me grow!" it sang with pride,
But it was just a stubborn little guide.

An oak rolled its eyes at the dandelion's flair,
"With all that fluff, you spread everywhere!"
While ivy laughed, climbing a pole,
"Not all heroes wear a flowered soul!"

The grass tickled the ants below,
"Watch your step; don't put on a show!"
Each blade held lore of the past so fun,
Tales of the mulch when the day was done.

In this kingdom where nature schemes,
All plants spin tales that tease our dreams.
With every rustle and cheeky grin,
Legends of green are where fun begins.

Moss-Covered Diaries

In a mossy nook, secrets are kept,
With petals and leaves where flowers have leapt.
Each whisper of green has a story to share,
Of blooms and bugs, dancing without a care.

A rose wrote a note to a clover once,
"You're luckier than me, you sassy little dunce!"
But clover just blushed, feeling quite shy,
"Don't worry, dear rose, we all reach the sky!"

Beneath the ferns, the earthworms write,
Of garden mischief in the cool moonlight.
With each squiggle, they tell a tale,
Of flower friendships that never grow stale.

In these diaries, laughter grows strong,
With funny stories that sing a sweet song.
Moss-covered pages witness all the fun,
Nature's own archives, where joy is spun.

Secrets of the Flowerbed

In the garden, gossip flows,
Blossoms share their silly woes.
Roses blushing, tulips tease,
Bumblebees buzz, aiming to please.

Daisies wink at passing ants,
Whispering secrets, doing a dance.
Sunflowers nod, with cheeky glee,
While violets giggle, sipping tea.

A dandelion dreams of flight,
While weeds plot mischief in the night.
Forget-me-nots forget to care,
As peonies play tag in the air.

So join the fun, come take a peek,
The garden's tales are quite unique.
With every bloom, a laugh, a jest,
In the flowerbed, life is best!

Stories Woven in Stem

Each stem holds a tale untold,
Of petals bold and stories old.
A sunflower's wink at the dawn,
While daisies dance, lustily drawn.

Lilies sigh, oh, such a life,
Avoiding gossip, avoiding strife.
Zinnias boast of colors bright,
While marigolds plot for spite.

The lavender laughs, all sweet and spry,
As wind carries tales that fly high.
Tulips cheer for the evening star,
Sharing secrets of who they are.

In every leaf, a joke resides,
Nature's humor, no need to hide.
With blooms so merry and stories grand,
Let laughter grow in every land!

Vibrant Echoes of Earth

From roots to blooms, the laughter spreads,
In vibrant echoes, the garden treads.
Snapdragons giggle, a fiery bunch,
While poppies sway, sharing lunch.

Garden gnomes with silly grins,
Join the jest as the fun begins.
Butterflies swirl like confetti bright,
While crickets chirp, filling the night.

Vegetables gossip in rows so neat,
Peas poke fun, waving their feet.
Even the soil has tales to share,
With worms composing a giggling fair.

So hear the echoes of laughter clear,
As nature plays, we all draw near.
In vibrant hues and silly seams,
The earth spins tales of joyful dreams!

Reflections in a Pond of Petals

In a pond where petals float,
Frogs croak out their little note.
Lilies laugh, a chorus swell,
As fish splash tales with a splashy yell.

The mirror smiles back, quite absurd,
Reflecting ripples, thoughts unheard.
Dragonflies dance in the sun's bright gaze,
While water striders play tag for days.

The moon dips low with a cheeky wink,
As frogs and flowers link up to drink.
Each moment a story, a giggling song,
In this whimsical world where all belong.

So lean into the laughter, let spirits soar,
In a pond of petals, there's always more.
With echoes of joy and funny delight,
Reflections in nature are pure and bright!

Threads of Color and Light

In a garden bright, a twist of fate,
A flower sneezed; oh, what a state!
With petals flying all around,
It painted the air without a sound.

A bee buzzed by, wearing a hat,
Sipping nectar, chatting with the cat.
Roses rolled their eyes with mirth,
As daisies danced across the earth.

Sunflowers spun in a dizzy swirl,
While tulips giggled, giving a twirl.
Each bloom told tales, so vivid and grand,
Of entertained bees and rabbits unplanned.

Laughter erupted, the leaves joined in,
Underneath the bright sun's cheerful grin.
Nature's fabric, a quilt of delight,
Threads of color and light, oh so bright!

The Flower's Legacy

Once a bloom with a dazzling name,
Declared its mission, seeking fame.
"I'll grow so tall, let the world know,
That I can dance, and I can glow!"

But daisies chuckled, "You'll trip for sure,
With roots so fine, it's hard to endure!"
Yet the brave flower stood firm and proud,
Waving its petals, garnering a crowd.

Pansies set up a circus show,
With a clowning bee and a juggling doe.
The legacy grew—not just one, but many,
Each bloom was chuckling, and there were plenty!

In the end, they all learned to share,
Fame's pretty neat, but fun is rare.
So they giggled and bloomed, a colorful spree,
A garden of laughter, wild and free!

Invocations of Petal Spirits

Gather 'round, oh blooms divine,
Let's conjure spirits with our vine.
Petal by petal, we raise the cheer,
Whispering secrets for all to hear.

A tulip twirled with utmost grace,
While lilacs giggled, rolling in place.
The petals whispered ancient lore,
Hoping to summon laughs galore.

"Come forth, dear spirits of floral tales,
Share with us your colorful gales!"
A butterfly sparked, and with a swoop,
Joined the petals in their goofy loop.

With a flick and a flutter, they swayed as one,
Creating magic, having such fun.
The garden filled with mirth and delight,
As petals danced beneath the moonlight.

A Symphony of Sprouts

In the soil, a sprout took a stand,
Waving its arms like a marching band.
"Let's form a symphony, oh what a sight!
We'll play our tunes both day and night!"

The carrots provided a deep bass sound,
While radishes twirled, all around.
Lettuce strummed on a leafy guitar,
And beans joined in from afar.

Broccoli chimed in like a regal king,
With beats so fresh, it made birds sing.
Together they played, a whimsical show,
Nature's orchestra, putting on a glow.

Rotating each night till the stars gleamed,
They danced in harmony, everyone dreamed.
In this garden, a tune took flight,
A symphony sprouted, oh so bright!

Unraveled Roots

In the garden, plants conspire,
To tell tales of their wiring.
Roses laughing, snickers bloom,
While daisies plot in the gloom.

Worms wear glasses, claim they see,
A path to freedom, oh so free!
Petunias gossip, marigolds smirk,
A botanical network at work.

Violets bet on who will sprout,
While tulips dance, they twist about.
A sprout so proud, claims the crown,
But crickets chirp, "Hey, sit down!"

As the sun sets, shadows grow,
Plants pack up for the show.
With roots intertwined, they laugh some more,
A garden's ball, never a bore.

Time Captured in Bloom

Oh, how time flies in the plot,
With petals spinning like a robot.
Daisies laugh, a clock's precision,
While sunflowers claim to know the season.

The clock ticks slow for roses bright,
While violets drift, out of sight.
"Is it noon or is it night?"
Bud says, "Who cares, it feels just right!"

Bees arrive in formal wear,
Mixing honey, without a care.
Lilies shout, "What's the rush?"
While thistles mutter, "Oh, hush, hush!"

As hours dance on petals' tips,
Time captures laughter in their grips.
With every bloom, a tick-tock song,
In the flower bed, we all belong.

The Blooming Aftermath

After the shower, blooms appear,
Petals glisten, oh dear, oh dear!
But wait, what's that? A snail parade!
Taking notes on how to invade!

Tulips giggle, "Look at them crawl!"
While pansies roll, "They'll never stand tall!"
A butterfly blinks in surprise,
At the sight of such a bizarre prize.

Worms wear hats, looking quite dapper,
"It's a social event," they happily chapper.
Petunias sigh, "What's with the fuss?"
Hoping the slugs don't make a fuss.

As chaos blooms in the soft, wet dirt,
A sunflower shrieks, "Oh, that's gonna hurt!"
With laughter shared in the aftermath,
A garden's tale, a comedic path.

Shades of Resilience

In bright hues, we stand so tall,
While stubborn weeds take the fall.
Dandelions boast of their grit,
"Resilience is my favorite fit!"

Petals strut in vibrant shades,
Crickets leap, playing charades.
"Who's the strongest?" they all decree,
"Let's have a dance-off, just wait and see!"

The sunset bathes us all in gold,
A garden story waiting to be told.
With roots so deep and smiles wide,
In life's garden, we take pride.

Through storm and sun, we find our cheer,
Blossoming together, year after year.
With laughter echoing through the air,
In shades of resilience, we all share!

Memory Woven in Blossoms

In a garden where daisies dance,
I lost my shoe during a prance.
Now I hop like a cheerful frog,
While neighbors laugh at my wet sock.

The roses gossip about my plight,
They sneak peeks, then take flight.
Tulips giggle, waving hello,
As I bumble through the flower show.

Each petal holds a silly tale,
Of escapades that never pale.
The bees buzz loud, my secret fans,
They cheer me on with tiny plans.

With blossoms bright, my heart does sing,
In this garden, life's a funny thing.
The memories grow like wild vines,
Twisting in humorous designs.

The Heartbeat of a Faded Garden

In a yard where humor blooms,
Worn-out tools and rich perfumes.
A squirrel stole my last ripe pear,
Now he's the neighborhood's millionaire!

The daisies argue on who is best,
While weeds wear crowns, never stressed.
The sun is shining just for me,
While shadows play hide-and-seek with glee.

The lilies laugh at my green thumb,
As I trip over a garden drum.
With every fall, the peonies cheer,
"Get up, dear friend! Let's sip some beer!"

In this garden of tangled mirth,
Where every plant dances with worth,
Life's heartbeat echoes, quirky and grand,
Crafting folly in this fertile land.

A Bloom for Every Whisper

Whispers float like petals in air,
Secrets shared without a care.
The daisies nod, ever so wise,
As bees wear tiny, buzzing ties.

A tulip told me a joke so sweet,
About a rose with two left feet.
The sunflowers laughed till they cried,
While butterflies danced side by side.

Each laugh sparks a blooming spree,
As I plant laughs under the tree.
With every chuckle, roots entwine,
Creating humor in every line.

A garden full of joyous tricks,
Where even the bumblebees do flicks.
So come and join this giggling crew,
In a world where laughter is always new.

Reflections on a Petaled Journey

In gardens bright and wide,
A petal took a slide,
It danced upon a breeze,
While chuckling with the trees.

It bumped into a bee,
Who buzzed with glee,
"You're such a silly bloom,
What brings you here, to zoom?"

A raindrop joined the play,
And splashed in disarray,
"Oh dear, we're getting drenched!
Let's leap before we're clenched!"

With laughter all around,
They swirled upon the ground,
A petaled journey spun,
In nature's crazy fun.

The Elegy of the Stalwart Stem

A stem stood proud, quite tall,
Until it tripped and fall,
"Oh dear! What a mishap!"
It cried, while taking a nap.

The ground laughed, quite amused,
"Look at you! So confused!
With roots that seek the dirt,
You've now become a shirt!"

A ladybug appeared,
With giggles, it cheered,
"Get up, you clumsy mate!
Let's have some fun, don't wait!"

So, the stem shook its leaves,
And laughed till it believes,
That falling's not so grim,
When laughter's in the whim.

Tales of Resilience in Bloom

In gardens where we stand,
Stories sprout from the land,
A blossom tells of strife,
And how it found its life.

"Once I was just a seed,
A champion of the creed,
I sprouted through the cracks,
With strength that never lacks!"

The daisies chimed in cheer,
"Standing tall, have no fear!
We can weather any storm,
And still remain so warm!"

A breeze of tales did roll,
With each petal, a goal,
In unity, they bloomed,
And filled the garden's room.

When Flowers Speak Softly

When petals whisper low,
The garden starts to glow,
"Did you hear what I said?"
The rose gently spread.

"I thought I heard a pun!
Was it the sunflower run?"
They giggled in delight,
As crickets joined the fight.

"A daisy made a joke,
About a silly oak,
He said, 'I'm feeling blue!'
And everyone just knew!"

While petals laughed aloud,
The sun peeked from a cloud,
A bloom with humor bright,
Turned the day into night.

A Daffodil's Tale

In a garden bright, a daffodil
With dreams of sprouting wings to fulfill,
Told jokes to bees, they buzzed with glee,
Spreading laughter through the leafy spree.

One sunny day, he dressed in gold,
A fashionista, if truth be told,
But a squirrel laughed, 'You're just a stem!'
He muttered back, 'At least I'm not them!'

With petals wide, he danced on breeze,
Claiming charm, he'd do as he pleased,
But clouds above, they rumbled with pride,
'You'll wilt and fade; no need to hide!'

Yet still he laughed, with petals aglow,
For every moment is a free show,
And under the sun, he twirled around,
A daffodil king, without a crown.

Transience of Beauty

A rose once sighed, 'I'm here today,
But watch me wither, I must say,
What's the point of all this flair?
When soon I'll tumble—who'll even care?'

The daisies giggled, 'Don't be a fool,
We bloom and fade, but that's the rule,
Embrace the sun; it's not a race,
We flower quickly, let's celebrate space!'

Yet a tulip chimed, 'But look at me,
In spring I'm mighty, like a bee,
Then summer comes, and I am dashed,
Oh, what a ride, it's gone so fast!'

Still, they all laughed, sharing their fate,
In petals bright, they chose to create,
A fleeting moment worth a cheer,
For beauty blooms, then disappears.

Blossoms of Tomorrow

In a meadow ripe, young buds declare,
'Stomorrow's bloom will be beyond compare!'
They dream of hues, of vibrant sights,
And plot their fashion for spring delights.

A sunflower plotted with some glee,
'Watch me tower over all, you'll see!
Though raindrops fall, I will stand tall,
A bright golden crown to outshine them all!'

The violets whispered, 'What a dream!
But yesterday's blooms had quite the gleam,
We'll wear our colors, oh so bright,
And dance through the day, 'till the night!'

So blossoms laughed, and with a cheer,
'Let's flaunt our petals, oh, never fear!
For tomorrow waits with colors anew,
And nature's laugh is always true!'.

When Flowers Remember

A chrysanthemum sat with a frown,
'What was I thinking, dressing in brown?'
The pansies giggled, 'You're still a peach,
And colorful stories are what we teach!'

They recalled the time a bee wore shades,
Buzzing around, in laughter he played,
While roses blushed, with petals aglow,
They hummed, 'Oh dear, how cute that show!'

The lilies sighed, 'Remember the rain?
We danced like children, so wild, so plain,
The puddles formed, we splashed around,
In joyful chaos, the fun was profound!'

So as they shared tales of swirling past,
Each flower found a joy that would last,
For in the garden, both vivid and bright,
Memories bloom in rays of light.

Petals of Time

In a garden where laughter grows,
A flower forgot which way it goes.
It danced in circles, round and round,
While bees just stared, lost and found.

With each tick-tock, it swayed its head,
Thinking of dreams, half-slept and shed.
The sun just chuckled, a bright yellow grin,
As petals fell off, but jokes would begin.

A ladybug said, 'Why so puffy?'
'I'm just a cloud, feeling quite fluffy!'
The daisy rolled over with a big laugh,
'Oh dear petals, you're quite the gaffe!'

So under the sky, they share a jest,
In this garden, they're simply blessed.
For time may tick in its usual way,
But here, it's all about the play!

Whispers in Bloom

In a patch where gossip softly hums,
The tulips chatter, discussing their bums.
'Oh, darling rose, your scent's so divine!'
'But your thorns, sweetie, they aren't hard to find.'

The marigolds giggle, their heads held high,
With petals all orange, they reach for the sky.
They whisper of secrets, of bugs and the sun,
Of pollen parties that are simply fun.

A dandy dandelion, proud as can be,
Said, 'I'm not a weed; I'm wild and free!'
But bees just buzzed, 'You're all fluff, no style,'
And the garden erupted in laughter and smiles.

So next time you stroll past that colorful plume,
Remember the flowers, the joy in their bloom.
For in their small world, they cherish the fun,
With laughs and with whispers, they're never done!

A Tapestry of Colors

A patchwork of petals on the hillside bright,
Each hue telling tales in the golden light.
'Why is the violet so shy,' one asked,
'Oh, darling, she's just got a quirky task!'

The orange marigold jumped in with cheer,
'Let's paint the world, have no fear!'
But the bluebells rang out, 'We're delicate too!'
'Oh, hush your tones, let's all be true!'

'We're not just pretty; we have wit!'
The cosmos winked, feeling quite lit.
So, let's dance to the rhythm of spring,
A tapestry of laughter is what we bring!

In this garden of humor, where colors collide,
Every bloom shares a giggle, with joy as our guide.
And when people pass by, they'll stop and they'll stare,
For nature's ballet is too much to bear!

Secrets Beneath the Stem

Beneath the surface, there's gossip galore,
What do flowers whisper when no one's ashore?
The daisies reveal their roots in a knot,
While sunflowers boast of the sun's warm spot.

Down in the soil, it's a wild soirée,
With fungi and critters coming out to play.
They share their stories, laugh through the night,
As the earthworms twist with sheer delight.

'I've seen a bee trip over a petal!'
Said one sneaky root, chuckling a little.
'The poor thing fell, but oh what a sight,
Nature's own blooper in the pale moonlight!'

So if you listen closely, you might just hear,
The comical tales that everyone holds dear.
For under the stems, the secrets unite,
In the garden of giggles, all is just right!

The Poetry of Growth

In a garden where daisies jig,
Petunias twist and turn with a gig.
Their dreams are all lofty and sweet,
But they trip on their own little feet.

The tulips toast to the sun so bright,
While the weeds plot mischief, oh what a sight!
With laughter that spreads from stem to stem,
Who knew flowers could be so zen?

Between the Thorns

In the shade where the roses pout,
A busy bumblebee buzzes about.
He's searching for nectar, oh what a chase,
Accidentally tickling a cactus's face.

The thorns all chuckle; it's quite a show,
As the bee makes a quick, silly flow.
He dances around with a flair so bold,
While the flowers sip tea, their stories told.

Blossom Reveries

Underneath the bright moon's glow,
Petals whisper secrets, soft and slow.
A daffodil dreams of dancing free,
While daisies sway with exuberant glee.

The pansies don silly hats from the past,
Telling jokes of the world so vast.
With giggles that spring into the night air,
Who knew blooms could have such flair?

The Blooming Odyssey

A sunflower sails on a breeze of jest,
Plotting adventures, dreaming of the best.
With all of his friends, they set forth, bold,
For treasures of laughter and stories untold.

They frolic through fields where the wildflowers roam,
Knowing together, they've found a home.
With petals like sails and roots holding tight,
Their journey is hilariously bright!

The Silent Speaker of Gardens

In the garden, whispers flow,
Plants gossip while we don't know.
Tulips giggle, daisies tease,
Sunflowers strut, they aim to please.

Roses roll their eyes in bloom,
Petals sigh, they're all in tune.
Bees buzz jokes, while ants all laugh,
Nature's tale is quite the gaff.

A squirrel mimics a gardener's sway,
Sneaking snacks, oh what a play!
With each bloom, a jest unfolds,
In this plot, it's pure gold.

So next time you stroll through green,
Remember the laughs that go unseen.
For in the silence, joy does thrive,
In gardens where all flowers jive.

Stories Woven in Bloom

In a patch of petals, secrets hum,
Laughing lilies, oh so glum.
Dandelions weave tales of flight,
While violets giggle, what a sight!

Pansies wink in the soft sunlight,
Yelling jokes only flowers find right.
Roses blush, but too much fame,
They're tired of the teasing name game.

A bumblebee's buzz is full of cheer,
Tickled by pollen that's always near.
With every breeze, a plot is spun,
In this garden, we all have fun.

So gather 'round, both flower and bee,
In this lively tale of glee.
Where blossoms bloom with laughter vast,
Their stories, a riot to outlast.

Flowers Unfolding in Verse

A petal twirls with a silly grin,
Speaking tales of pollen win.
Snapdragons snap, what a charade,
While marigolds dance in the shade.

In sunlit corners, laughter rings,
Butterflies flit, sharing their flings.
Daisies chuckle, waving goodbye,
While close by, sun's fierce eye.

Hydrangeas gossip, spilling the tea,
"Did you see that?" "Oh, let it be!"
Petunias puff, proud they stand tall,
While daisies do the chicken dance, y'all!

So when you're near this floral stage,
Remember each bloom plays its page.
For in every bud, a jest is found,
In gardens where laughter knows no bound.

Palette of Nature's Serenade

In fields of color, laughter sparks,
Where roses play in leafy parks.
A daffodil trips, such a surprise,
A poppy in stitches, oh how it cries!

Through the tulips, a breeze does tease,
Giggling daisies dance with ease.
Ferns whisper 'round, thinking they're sly,
Chasing butterflies as they float by.

In this canvas of vibrant hue,
Each bloom has a tale, fresh and new.
With every petal that opens wide,
A canvas of humor, we can't hide.

So paint the day with flower's cheer,
Laugh with nature, hold it dear.
For joy in gardens, truly leads,
To brighter paths and silly deeds.

The Language of the Unsung Blossom

In gardens filled with laughter, blooms do sway,
Petals gossip secrets, in a flowery way.
Daisy whispers to Rose, 'You smell quite grand!'
Meanwhile, Sunflower winks, 'Get a tan, my friend!'

Tulip tells a joke, it falls flat on the ground,
While Lavender hums tunes, a sweet, fragrant sound.
Pansy rolls her eyes, says, 'Oh please, how dire! '
Jokes from a blossom could set hearts on fire!

But still they jostle, in breezy delight,
Each bloom a character, in nature's light.
The shy ones giggle, the bold ones laugh loud,
Together they form quite the floral crowd!

So next time you wander near blossoms so fine,
Remember their antics, just like yours and mine.
For in each petal, there's a tale to unfold,
In the chatter of flowers, humor shines bold.

Threads of Fragrance and Time

A daffodil danced, twirling 'round with glee,
Said, 'Watch me, folks! I'm the rockstar of the spree!'
But Lily chimed in, 'You think you're so bright,
Just wait 'til Oregano shows up tonight!'

The daisies rolled laughter, waving their heads,
As the violets took turns in their fanciful beds.
'When do we blossom with pride and with cheer?'
'Tomorrow,' said Fern, 'I'll bring snacks, never fear!'

The wind blew a tickle, the petals all shook,
Said Rose with a smirk, 'I'll go write a book!
Of love and of longing, of roses and thyme,
That's it! I'm a poet; I need some lime!'

With colors ablaze and stories to share,
Life is a garden, with laughter to spare.
A scent of adventure wafts thick in the air,
Come join in the fun, there's joy everywhere!

Portraits of a Floral Odyssey

In the heart of the meadow, a flower parade,
With Marigold shining, and dandelions displayed.
'I'm the star of the show!' claimed the prancing Snap,
But forget-me-not winked, 'Don't take a nap!'

Zinnias in costumes, ready to prance,
They've practiced their moves, oh, just watch their dance!

'Whose turn is it now?' shouted Peony bold,
'It's time for our stories, let them unfold!'

With petals a-flutter and colors galore,
Each bloom brings a chuckle, each chuckle a roar.
Chrysanthemum giggled, 'Why did Bee cross the road?
To get to the hive, where the wild honey flowed!'

So they jammed in the sun, basked in sweet cheer,
Creating bright memories, year after year.
For in every blossom, tales of joy dwell,
In this riot of color, laughter rings like a bell!

Blooming in Shadows

In the shade of the trees, where shy blossoms bloom,
Whispering secrets, dispelling the gloom.
Beggars can't be choosers, said the timid Fern,
While tiny violets plotted, 'It's our chance to learn!'

With wise old Oak keeping watch over the game,
Each quiet petal played, never seeking fame.
'Let's throw a party!' shouted bold Moss so spry,
With winter's chill fading, it's time we all fly!

The décor was lovely, with twigs and some dew,
When a dainty lawn sprite crashed in, just for a view.
She spun them round, flaring laughter on high,
And under starlit shadows, their giggles would fly!

So bloom in the shadows, where humor takes root,
Each leaf tells a tale, each laughter a hoot.
In the wild world of flora, where quirks intertwine,
Every petal a jest, every branch a good time!

Unwritten Verses of Nature's Ink

In the garden, blooms debate,
A daisy claims it's never late.
A tulip laughs, with all its might,
"At least I don't have to bud goodnight!"

The rose, it poses in the sun,
"I'm the fairest, oh what fun!"
But with a thorn, it caused a rift,
Now every bloom must watch their gift.

A bee swoops down, with sweet intent,
"Do I steal nectar? No way, just rent!"
The petals giggle, a lovely sight,
Nature's jesters, day and night!

But rainclouds frown, a piece of shade,
"Where's the humor? I'm just made!"
The flowers shrug in petals bright,
"Chill out, dear cloud, it's all alright!"

In the Embrace of Fragrant Tales

A daffodil once told a lie,
"I'm a sunbeam, I can fly!"
A nearby rose just rolled its eyes,
"Oh please, don't hit us with your highs!"

The garden gnome, he took a seat,
"In my pot, I find a treat!"
But mice ran past, in quite a blur,
"Watch out, watch out, here comes the fur!"

One night a moonbeam came to play,
Whispering secrets at the end of day.
"Oh floppy petals, can you see?"
"I've seen the world, it's wild and free!"

In fragrant tales, they laugh and roll,
Each cheeky bloom has its own goal.
A garden filled with fun-filled cheer,
With laughter ringing loud and clear!

The Dances of Petals and Time

Petals waltz in soft spring air,
Dancing round, without a care.
A bumblebee brings jazzy tunes,
While flowers sway beneath the moons.

But who stepped on the poor crocus?
"That's not how you do a focus!"
The daisy giggles, and takes a twirl,
"Come, my friends, let's give it a whirl!"

The daisies wear their hats in style,
Each one competing with a smile.
The lilacs chuckle, having fun,
"Your hats are silly, mine's a bun!"

In this jolly dance of time,
Each petal slips into a rhyme.
With laughter echoing, hearts are light,
In nature's ball, everything's bright!

Fables of the Unseen Garden

In a patch where shadows loom,
Socks and shoes find little room.
A rabbit hops, decked in a hat,
"I'm more fashionable than a cat!"

The flowers gossip, oh what fun,
"Who wore the best dress in the sun?"
A peony made just one complaint,
"Those petals are loud, I need a paint!"

A ladybug joins in to sway,
"In spots or stripes, I shine all day!"
The flowers cheer, a raucous shout,
"In our garden, there's never doubt!"

And as the sun dips down to rest,
The unseen garden feels so blessed.
With laughter, cheer, and tales unfold,
In every petal, a story told!

Shadows of a Flower

In the garden, blooms so bright,
A shadow sneezes, oh what a fright!
Petals giggle, a dance they make,
With every wind, new jokes they take.

Sunflower whispers a shady pun,
While daisies laugh and have their fun.
Roses roll their eyes with flair,
'We won't be outdone, we have our share!'

Tulips trade quips, oh what a scene,
A riot of colors, like a dream.
Behind the leaves, a bee dons shades,
As laughter buzzes in sunlit glades.

So if you wander among the blooms,
Pack a smile, dispel those glooms.
For flowers know, in a world so dire,
A sprinkle of humor can light a fire!

Inked in Bloom

In a sketchbook, scented dreams reside,
Petals doodle, nowhere to hide.
A cactus tries to pose for fame,
But ends up with ink, oh what a shame!

A daffodil blushes, ink on its face,
'This isn't the style I'd thought to embrace!'
Marigold giggles, 'You're just a mess,'
But each stain adds charm, I must confess.

Violets rhyme, with ink-stained paws,
'Let's start a brand, we'll be the cause!'
Pansies join in, with colors so wild,
Creating a book, Bloom's own wild child.

Each brushstroke sings, a laughter-infused tale,
Of flowers bold, who refuse to pale.
In a garden where art meets the whimsy of spring,
Every petal's a story waiting to sing!

Chronicles of the Heart's Bloom

In a meadow where hearts collide,
A tulip's secret it cannot abide.
With whispers sweet, it starts a tale,
Of love that blossoms despite the frail.

A daisy's crush on a bee so grand,
Pollination dreams, oh isn't it planned!
But the bee just buzzes, too busy to see,
While daisies plot mischief beneath the tree.

Lilies roll dice, playing fate with glee,
Hoping for love in the charm of the spree.
Cupid in bloom, with arrows so bright,
Helping the flowers find love in the night.

Yet laughter rings out, as puns take flight,
'Love's a garden, but who pulls it right?'
So gather the blooms, one joke at a time,
In the heart's odd garden, love's always in rhyme!

The Dance of Floral Seasons

In springtime's ball, flowers take their cue,
Tulips twirl with a sweet rendezvous.
Daisies skip in a cheerful dance,
While violets giggle, lost in romance.

Summer's here, oh what a fun spree,
Sunflowers sway, as bold as can be.
Petunias prance in the warm sunlight,
While crickets chirp, joining the delight.

Autumn arrives, with a crackling sound,
Flowers gossip as leaves spin round.
Chrysanthemums strut, dressed like queens,
While marigolds share juicy scenes.

Winter lingers, but blooms don't freeze,
With laughter echoing in the brisk breeze.
A snowdrop grins, with petals so white,
'In every season, we share our light!'

www.ingramcontent.com/pod-product-compliance
Lightning Source LLC
Chambersburg PA
CBHW071814160426
43209CB00003B/79